The Springtime Of Life

A Journey in Verse

Shashwati Srivastava

BookLeaf
Publishing

India | USA | UK

Made with ❤ on the BookLeaf Publishing Platform
www.bookleafpub.in
www.bookleafpub.com

Dedication

To my parents,
Sudha and Ghanshyam Murari Srivastava
who gave me their creative, literary genes.

And

To Abhishek,
the ever flowing ink in my pen.

Preface

It is a tough task to encapsulate the journey of writing a book, especially when it is punctuated by long pauses.

This book is a collection of poems that remained as stray writings over the years. Some were written when I was a student at University of Delhi, and later at Jawaharlal Nehru University. Others have been written at various stages and in different locations that have stirred my inner poet into creative reflection. However, they are not presented in chronological order in this book.

These poems are an expression of my personal experiences with the people, places and breathtaking natural beauty I have encountered over the years till now. This includes not just my birthplace but also the places I have lived in or had the pleasure of visiting.

It is also a chronicle of fond memories that I wanted to capture and preserve for posterity; a scrap book in verse of vibrant images, vivid moments and lyrical, melodious soundscapes. The images I have tried to recapture and revisit through these poems are not just of my own country. There are also mementoes of my stay in Australia and all that I encountered there.

Some of these experiences have stunned me with their depth of emotion, while others have subtly changed me in ways that I realised only later. Throughout this journey of compiling my previous work and adding new poems to their number, I have realised that there is poetry in the simplest of things. A child's guileless laughter, the aroma of mother's cooking, or bunch of squirrels arguing loudly— all have hidden verses waiting to be discovered. All it needs is a sensitive pen and an observant eye.

This book is a compilation of my discovery of these hidden words, recovered from various corners of life and crevices of nature. It is my interpretation of the truths I have lived and the emotions I have felt. I share these with you with hope and gratitude.

Shashwati Srivastava

Vijayawada,
April 2025

Acknowledgements

There are many who have been with me throughout the journey of bringing this book to life. I would like to express my gratitude to all of them.

I am eternally grateful to my mother and father for imbuing in me an abiding love for the written word. To them also is the credit for fanning the creative spirit within me, and for inculcating an appreciation for good literature. They are my harshest and wisest critics and also my loudest cheerleaders.

I am extremely thankful to my husband Abhishek for sharing my dream of seeing my name in print. He first spotted the kernels of this book within me, and egged me on towards completing it. I greatly appreciate him for his unique mind, wise counsel, strong opinions and unwavering support. His periodic questioning and analysis of my work also provided me with new perspectives of looking at the world around me. I am especially grateful to him for hearing out the loud ramblings of an exhausted wife and mother in the throes of putting together her first book!

My children are the brightest lights of my life, without whom I would be lost and incomplete. Thank you Abhidha and Akshobhya for your (seemingly) throwaway lines and innovative questions that have always sparked new ideas in me. I am specially thankful to my dear daughter Abhidha for sharing her wonderful photograph of Manali (Himachal Pradesh) that adorns the cover of this book.

My in-laws and my sister have always been my strongest supporters in every new venture that I have undertaken. I deeply appreciate their unwavering faith in my abilities.

Finally, Thank you to the team of Bookleaf Publishing for helping me make this book a reality.

That Night

Rain,
Unrelenting tireless
Torrential rain.
Rapping the window pane;
molten silver
flecks of mercury
Incandescent moonlight
Cloud-ringed moon.
The wolves call...
glow worms are out
Iridescent, little moons.
Smoky, mystic whiteness
moaning winds
Creaking doors
Trilling wind chimes.
Fear. Frozen voices
Constricted throats
Flickering lights...
Then Darkness.
Huddled , curled up in bed,

Apprehensive
Wakeful
I lay watching
The unknown
The occult
The sheer witchcraft of the night.

Rhythm of the Rain

Listen to the rhythm of the falling rain,
Drumming a steady staccato beat on the tin.
Tap tap tapping in triple time frenzy,
On the foggy glass of my windowpanes.
A loud, baleful rumble as cloud cymbals crash,
A gentle gurgle as the drops touch the grass.
A startled 'plop! ' from flowers in deep slumber.
The splashy exclamation of disturbed standing water,
Or the drenching declaration of a agitated puddle
Forced out of shape by a speeding vehicle,
Single-mindedly focussed on getting home.

Listen to the rhythm of the falling rain,
A soft murmur as its anger recedes.
The downpour now a burbling hiss.
The cymbals replaced by a mild caressing wind,
The drops a whisper on the damp pavement.
A gentle drizzle jumping off the leaves
From one to the other like escaping thieves.
Till it finally comes to hide, or perhaps rest,

On blades of grass or floral nest.
Each gentle droplet a pearl drawn in light
Broken bits of sunlight, a rainbow bright.
And then the hushed stillness,
Of a landscape refreshed.
Cleansed of impurities,
The summer's thirst quenched.

The Window

A square shaft of light,
Enters through the window.
Dust swirling in its wake
Gold flecks dancing to a cosmic tune.
Freshness, warmth, radiance
Chase out the cold, damp, gloom.
Banish the sense of impending doom.

Hope is unleashed
Ideas freed, evenly balanced
intellect unbound. Feelings serene.
Thoughts glimmer and flicker
A kaleidoscope of emotions flit across,
Silhouettes form, reform, reshape.

A flood of sentiment swirls through the recesses,
A rush of novel solicitude,
Washing it all away
in a mysterious cleansing ritual.
A strange sacrament of regeneration.

I am tossed in a sea of truth,
And then washed ashore...
Drenched in self- belief,
Soaked to the skin in the elixir of fortitude,
Imagination abloom, intellect aglow
Salting the blandness of existence.
Mouth agape, head a-wonder, awash in
The miracles wrought by an open mind.

To Her... Ode to a Poem

Dancing eyes, mischief lurking.
Pert nose wrinkled in concentration.
A naughty smile playing hide and seek,
Amid rosebud lips as they move to speak.

A bright spark brimming with promise,
My ray of sunshine banishing dark skies.
The reason I am, I want to be.
The tinkle of her laughter,
The spring in my step.
The truth in her eyes,
The colours of my soul
Her sparkling wit
The light of my spirit.
A beautiful mind,
Creative and enquiring.
A blithe spirit,
who cares quietly.

You

Inspire me to try the unattempted.
Take a leap of faith
Teach me to battle the odds
armed with a smile and unshakeable will.
Show me that restrictions don't define us,
That strength comes from within,
No hurdle is too high
and no setback too hard.
Even the unsurmountable can be climbed
the complex simplified.
Only the path changes,
not the goal.

You
My perfect poem, deep with meaning.
Known by all, introduction not needing.
Friend, daughter, wise counsel, light,
A delicate bloom in the garden of delight.

Threshold

Is it a beginning?
Or is it an end point?
The cusp of something new
A portal to limitlessness.
On the very edge of time,
The verge of a discovery,
Or a lifetime left behind ?

Four very high inches,
An insurmountable obstacle,
An unclimbable cliff.
That craggy peak, beckoning, but difficult to scale.
A surreal realm, a twilight zone
Meeting point of the known and unknown.

Where comfort and discomfort collide,
Progress and stagnation battle.
A liminal space, heavy with obfuscation
Teetering between decision and hesitation
Yet on the brink of a resolution.

And when that peak is scaled, the mountain climbed,
Novel ideas awaken, light up the mind.
Fresh vistas beckon,
New adventures await.
Faith, strength and willpower my Companions
As new horizons and perspectives lie in wait.

A Child's Mind

Once, I tried to find,
What goes on in a child's mind?
T'was a bit dark, but mostly light
Colourful, sparkly, blindingly bright.
A spacious and yet narrow tunnel
Drawing me in like a Magic funnel.

Cheery, guileless laughter ringing loud,
A new thing learnt, a smile proud.
Memories of time in a warm, soft nest,
With mother's love-blood surrounded and blessed.

Myriad ideas, bubbling and swirling,
A rainbow of stories, imagined but sterling.
Thrilling games — small and great,
patiently waiting to be played.

Naughty tricks and mischief brewing,
A pink sun and blue cat crowing.
Cars flying, aeroplanes rowing,

Trees that talk and flowers glowing.
A chocolate river, a Lego house,
Filled with toys and books to browse.

No dark devilry; none at all.
Just a beautiful mind, standing tall.
A clear heart, with thoughts so pure,
And honesty and frankness that endure.

A blank slate, awaiting writing,
A soft sponge soaking up everything.
A unique miracle, one-of-a-kind spirit,
Director, actor, writer of his own script.
Marvellous teachers, I tell you truly,
Experts in the art of living fully.

Choices

A whisper of dawn breaks,
But shadows still dance.
The decision hangs heavy
Between fate and chance.

Is it a beginning; Or the denouement, endpoint?
Each heartbeat a question,
Every breath amid contention.
Echoes of unbridled laughter
Splash of poignant briny tears;
One evanescent moment
Encompassing a lifetime's hopes and fears.

Is it the mighty sun rising,
or twilight's gentle, hushed call?
Do we look towards the future
Or dwell in the fall?
Do we forget and forgive?
Or continue to wallow,
In ideas mean and revenge shallow?

Do we smile and shrug away the pain?
Or drown in melancholy,
Mind a storm and eyes rain?
Do we crumble and fragment like delicate glass,
Or fortify and harden with every tough ask?

The paths we walk, the words we say,
The actions taken everyday;
Aspiration, intention purpose chosen,
Define us clearly among the dozens.
Like yarn they weave a pattern bright,
Showing who we are in true light.

Mystique of the Mountains

Giants of stone, in deep slumber they lie
Robed in white beneath the cloudless sky.
A magical realm where frozen stillness reins
And sunlit peaks tower over earthly taints.

The crisp air bites, a nip sharp and keen
Golden sunlight now a dazzling silver sheen.
Each jagged edge, Gaia's sculpted art,
Drawing every gaze, stunning every heart.

Craggy faces hiding myriad tales of yore,
Or, perhaps memories of those who ventured before.
Stories of bears, leopards in the snow,
Or Yetis in caves, lurking in shadow?

The lure of heights, unbekanntes terrain,
Calls the intrepid with challenge to ascend.
Pristine slopes in graceful sharp curves extend,
Captivating with promise of snowman and sled.

The soft whisper of wind through icy lair
A wondrous feel beyond all compare.
A cottage teeming with rhododendrons,
Orchids, floral beauty and birdsongs.

Hot coffee mornings, breaths clouding,
Snow white views to the sundeck calling.
A gurgling river frantically rushing by,
Path hidden amid trees like a well-trained spy.

Trees laden with fruit, nature's bounty,
Exquisite treasures innumerable, uncounted.
Timeless grace, forever made to last;
Ethereal allure that holds us fast.

An Underwater Odyssey

Turquoise shallows give way to sapphire deep,
Sun's fractured rays in dancing patterns leap.
An enchanted world unfolds before my eyes,
Where coral castles and kelp forests rise.

Anemones sway, with clownfish darting near,
A playful ballet, delightful and dear.
Angelfish and Dory, a flash of blue and gold,
Parrotfish chomping, a story to be told.

Atolls and reefs a labyrinthine maze;
Here sponges stretch on languorous sunlit days.
A gentle giant, a sea turtle glides by,
Ancient wisdom shining in its wise eyes.

Sea fans unfurl like intricate lace,
Vibrant Starfish dot this aquatic space.
Clams and oysters with luminous secrets to hide,
Slumber quietly till the time is right.

What a wondrous world beneath crashing waves!
Azure landscape beckoning the brave.
An ancient chest, a shipwreck so old,
Nestles in the sea bed, still and cold.

Rickety, weedy what mysteries it holds!
And memories of voyages long and bold.
Tread carefully, masked explorer, and do not disturb,
For the sea has a million tales yet untold.

In Your Company

A surging stream of ideas flows,
Unlimited objectives, ideas beckon;
The impossible becomes easy
And the implacable suddenly meek.

Doubts are banished, possibilities unlocked;
Obstacles mere trifles, hurdles knocked out.
Darkness illuminated, golden light everywhere.
Heart unstifled, overjoyed beyond compare.

Over bright cheerful skies in glee it soars ,
Undaunted, unafraid of whatever lies in store.
Soft rose petals or prickly thorns,
Unbreakable mind, unshakeable to the core.

You. paper, pen and ink
Validator, affirmer for ideas on the brink.
Inspiration, Perspiration, energy, drive,
The orchard where unbridled imagination thrives.

The garden where individuality grows,
The gushing waterfall where artistry flows.
The stubborn rock against the tide,
A haven of comfort soft besides.

A Sunset in Canberra

Bold, bright brushstrokes,
Orange, red, purple, pink.
Splashed across the evening sky,
Smeared oe'er the blue ink.

A kohl-lined evening,
The sky in crimson- gold dressed;
Silhouettes and stories lurking,
What mysteries do they portend?

Delicate star-studded jewellery
In all its glory twinkling;
The moon a silver pendant,
Cosmic, warm and glowing.

The clouds are flowing tresses,
Untamed, wisps everywhere.
Sometimes swept up together,
Other times spread out bare.

And then the hushed murmurs,
As wild wind sweeps through the trees;
Whispering sweet endearments,
Rustling fervour in the leaves.

Then, She arrives softly,
Arrayed in scarlet splendour.
All eyes on her, the cynosure,
Transient, ephemeral, Belle of the ball.
Nightfall.

Bramhaputra

From mountainous heart, a silver ribbon alights,
Through craggy peaks it carves a path of might.
A glittering ribbon winding through the green
Under clear blue skies, a lush verdant scene.

Across borders, varied lands it spans,
Through sun-kissed plains, nations and clans.
Amid forests and hills and towns it glides,
Nourishing fields where fertile secrets hide.

But when the heavens pour, all hell breaks loose;
Its strained banks can no longer enclose.
A raging torrent, as fury takes hold,
A liquid beast, mighty, and bold.

As wrathful currents crash against shore,
Its gentle murmur turns into a roar.
Houses and trees in its wake are swept,
Man and beast equally bereft.

Both search for shelter when none abounds,
Both scramble up the higher grounds.
Just one strong current of the mighty in spate,
All it takes for Man and beast to be level, abreast.

When tranquility and calm return anew,
There's fruitful land and woodland profuse.
A primal power, unbound and free,
Finally surges to embrace the sea.

Seaside Musings

Fine ticklish grains smooth and cool,
As waves wash over little sandy pools.
Made of footprints yours and mine,
As azure skies preside over bright sunshine.

Sandcastles rise, with turrets proud and tall,
Then crumble softly as the wavelets maul.
Sea shells, critters little, long and wide,
Swim in and out with roaring tide.

Little red crabs, with sideways, scuttling stride,
And burrowing worms, their secrets nimbly hide.
The sandpipers dance, on slender, sprightly feet,
Searching for morsels, the ocean's salty treat.

The seagulls sonorous cry a song of joy,
A sea weary ship approaches, Land ahoy!
Fishing nets now reeled back in,
As the sun dips in golden sheen.

The tide's hushed murmur, a gentle lullaby,
As sandy bed glistens in sunset hues nearby.
A textured carpet, warm and deftly spun,
Where land and ocean, eternally are one.

Clouds

Cotton candy languidly floating,
Hidden sunshine over it gloating.
Multitude of shapes look me in the eye,
As I stare up into the sky.

A celestial rider astride fluffy horse,
Dragons, elephants, or a sea horse.
An ice cream cone to beat the heat,
Expressive faces in cloudy retreat.

White bright harbinger of light,
Grey, gloomy, banishing daylight.
Your moods fickle, as the wind blows,
When you gather, the storm grows.

Wrathful and fearsome in loud-voiced thunder,
Flashing sword of lightning strikes all asunder.
Wild wind howls, rushing to get away,
Ships go a-tossing, Reef the sails!

A glimmer of sun, returning calm,
Comforts the gentle rustle of the waving palm.
Earthy fresh fragrance lingering in the air,
As your billowy white brethren reappear.

Hanging as though in suspended animation,
Concealing woolly sheep and myriad formations.
Cool, moist caresses as they glide by,
Am I in the verandah or up in the sky?

Swirling gossamer beauties, a sight for sore eyes,
Travelling companions airy and light.
Messenger, passenger, a joy to behold,
Trove of legends, adventures untold.

Springtime of Life

Jocund spirit, fecund mind,
Ideas that no boundaries can confine.
Imagination that beyond the heavens soars,
Colourful, animated, with happiness galore.

What optimistic mindset, with positivity infinite!
When nothing looked impossible, and everything within
sight.
Heart so guileless, ingenuous and trusting,
Yet with mischief and whimsy bursting.

Fun and frolicsome, naïve and nice,
A sprightly mix of sugar and spice.
Days of laughter, games and sport,
When stories were long and worries short.

A time of simplicity and innocence,
Ah! the unforgettable days of juvenescence.
Transformative experiences that moulded us,
Loving encouragement that guided us.

Indulgent love, but well-directed displeasure,
That served to teach and imbue good manner.
Surprise outings, occasional gifts that brought untold joy,
Now fond memories preserved in a box of old toys.

A pile of vibrant storybooks, a few pages loose,
Bear testimony to banished bedtime blues.
A car with one wheel long ago mislaid,
Tale of races on smooth and rocky terrain.

A doll in red frock and ponytail golden,
At once a best friend and princess olden.
Sometimes a fairy with wings of glittery paper,
Other times a character in some imagined caper.

A little ball, building blocks of plastic,
Reminders of that timeless magic.
Such wonderful years, precious and cherished,
Childhood, an era angelic and unblemished.

Togetherness

Warm, sunny mornings spent in lazy recline,
As the aroma of fresh brewed coffee wafts in.
The restless rustling of fresh newsprint,
The smoothness of a well defined routine
Silences that sometimes speak volumes,
And sometimes confound with ambiguity.
Words rising and falling in tone and cadence,
A choreographed yet freestyle dance.
A crushing hug that chokes the heart,
A gentle pat that soothes and comforts.
Playful teasing, anxiety easing,
Togetherness is a pleasing feeling.

A heated discussion on matters small or big,
A wry smile preceding an admission of guilt.
Unspoken words brimming with meaning,
In eyes that glisten with deep feeling.
Unshed tears a carmine kohl
Burning eyes and searing the soul.

Then gentle fingers tousle the hair
A reassuring touch bringing comfort.
Life unimaginable without the other
The salt in tears, sugar in laughter.
Faith unwavering, support unceasing,
Togetherness is an empowering feeling.

Heartfelt laughter, smothered giggles
Trekking heights or awash in the sea.
Watching children build castles in the sand,
A moonlight walk hand in hand.
A hand held out when terrain is rough,
A motivating word when the going is tough.
Holidays, getaways refreshing and happy
A slew of memories, sacred and sublime.
Favourite melodies and arias deep with meaning,
Similarity in thoughts and rich with feeling.
Small gestures filled with infinite caring,
Togetherness is a passionate feeling.

A beauteous delicate fabric, soft as silk,
Crystal, glass, gossamer, camaraderie their ilk
An intricate firm structure, yet as easily broken
With hurt, neglect and words unpleasant.
A tiny plant to be nurtured with care,

Watered with affection, in love's sunshine rare.
Strong enough to withstand vagaries tiring,
Resilient in the face of circumstances challenging.
Bolstered by devotion and mutual understanding,
Togetherness is a responsible feeling.

The Retreat

My house on a hill top,
A river rippling at its feet,
Nimble fingers dancing across ivory keys,
Sweet strains of music wafting down the street.
Apricots and cherries waiting to fruit,
Apples, mangoes, oranges to boot.
Dewy mornings, sun soft and diffuse,
Honey and gold, warm and soothing
Igniting shadows orange and glowing.

While cottony wisps float lazily by,
Odd puffy ships in the cerulean sky.
Rosebuds nodding lips poised to speak,
A little hopping sparrow worm in its beak.
Crows cawing amid a songbird's call
Cool breeze teasing with rise and fall.
A cosy couch restful and inviting
Amid shady trees and dappled lighting.
Steaming brew and a favourite book,
Pleasant, relaxing, intimate nook.

Vibrant efflorescence verdant lawn
Where squirrels frolic in games unknown.

And when night falls with shadowy gloaming,
Crickets call, night owls go a roaming.
Moths find a rhythm around the lights,
Circling and stalling, sometimes flipping,
As milky moon floats, moonlight dripping.
The stars are a twinkle, nebulae aglow
Pinpricks of hope piercing the darkness below.
A generous velvet blanket comforting and snug,
My mind at rest, but with dreams agog.
Moonbeams streaming in through a window,
A feeling of safety, out of harm's way, secure.
Tranquil slumber smoothing out crinkles
Mind refreshed, paper sans wrinkles.

Till serene dawn breaks in a trilling chorus,
Birds, bees, man all back to business.
My house on a hill top,
A river rippling at its feet,
An oasis of calm amid bustling activity.
My haven, a sanctuary amid life's caprice,
A warm refuge, a revitalising retreat.

Sunrise in Vishakhapatnam

A hush, a soft grey breathing over the endless ocean.
The air, cool and salty, kisses my skin.
Raising ripples in the blue, yet tranquil within
An apricot blush appears, shy on horizon's blurred
cheek,
As grey turns azure and the moon gracefully retreats.
Fishermen, dark silhouettes on distant boats,
Embark on their perennial ride,
Casting nets into the still, dark water
Praying for bountiful catch and normal tide.
The apricot blush deepens to a fiery orange,
Streaking the sky in rose and gold hues.
Merchant ships approach, weary of the blue.
Looming over docks as they inch closer,
The long voyage is finally over.

A lone seagull cries, a sharp, clear note,
answered by another, and then many more.
Screaming, " it's time for arising and awakening.
No time to lose, Food's for the taking."

The sun, a molten coin, lifts free of the water's grasp,
Spilling golden light across the rippling expanse.
A misty curtain lifts, unveiling the hitherto unseen
The fishermen become clearer, their movements routine
Sailboats practice racing, backwash foaming en scene.

Joggers and walkers bobbing over the sand,
An old jetty creaks under sea's jouncing hand.
Sailors busy as Naval ships glitter and gleam,
Giant aquatic warriors, our protectors supreme.
Smell of seaweed, salty crisp breeze
Blue white and brown in a cosmic frieze.
Life's cup of joy full to the brim,
As dawn breaks o'er India's Eastern rim.
Waves of hope, energy, action in a rousing symphony,
As morning awakes in the City of Destiny.

Tabula Rasa

As black as the night
Yet white as the clouds,
As clear as crystal
As unsmudged as newly- made paper,
As pure as dew,
Bright as sunlight
and unfettered as bird in flight
Was life.

Till...
The ravages of time
The lines of experience
The vagaries of the world
The conflict of emotions
All came together and
left their mark.

Till...
The joys of sharing
The happiness of caring

The comfort of friendship
The warmth of true love
Were all obscured,
Eclipsed by a single master stroke.
With the ink of evil
The dye of lies
The colour of envy
The shadow of pride.

But hope springs eternal.
And so does perseverance
The circle was complete
Joys, sorrows,
Todays and tomorrows;
Love and true friends
Free rein and sunshine
All came back.
Overpowered the shadows
The Ogre vanquished.

The slate clean
All is set right and
The tabula rasa of my being is as it was
Unfettered, unshackled,
Pristine and unsmudged,
The stationery of God.

On Finding Myself

Sometimes in the soft pages of a well -thumbed book,
I find myself wandering, loitering around.
Looking for a reason to stay a while,
Or else, just be suspended in space and time.
As I stumble across the crisp petals of a dried rose,
I find a fragrant memory of lively days of yore.
A dog-eared page to mark the spot,
Where I once paused deep in thought.
A smudged fingerprint stained in ink blue,
Reminder of college work and scholarly pursuit.

Sometimes in the dark recesses of an old cookie tin,
I come across parts of my very being.
A snippet of joy from an accolade won,
A note of music from an oft rendered song.
A chunk of laughter at friendly jokes
And a sharp sliver of pain for those days bygone.
A sepia-tinted picture of grandparents dear,
Yet another of colourful yesteryear.

Sometimes in the pockets of a coat forgotten,
I rediscover romance and love again.
A silk kerchief with a lingering hint of spice,
A scrunched ball of paper, sweet nothings inside.
A long lost earring, one of a special pair,
A dry clump of grass from our special lair.
Dewy winter mornings and fresh brewed beans,
Snug smoky evenings illuminated by dancing flames.

Sometimes in the jumbled contents of a drawer,
I find thoughts I believed banished forever.
An old strip of tablets, a pain forgotten,
A small notebook of ruminations unbidden.
A balm to soothe an aching head,
A colourful picture in my child's hand.
A loving missive made by tiny hands,
Received on a birthday, or Mother's day, perchance.
Small red pieces of modelling clay,
Little hearts and diamonds made in play.
A frayed bracelet made of beads,
A special little girl's affectionate deed.

Sorted and cleaned and neatly arrayed,
All together they complete a portrait.

Or maybe, improve on one already painted,
That needed restoring, for ''twas a bit tainted.
Old, faded, yet loved unabashedly,
They came together and revived me.

Mother

A love boundless, across time and space,
A will so strong that can move mountains,
Faith so deep that it can't be fathomed,
Reserves of strength that appear hidden,
But can be accessed at once unbidden.
The calming hand to quiet all fears,
The soft, gentle touch that wipes away tears.
The soothing tones that lull to sleep,
The booming voice if anyone makes us weep.

Safe haven in all life's storms.
Teacher of good values and norms.
A gentle caress when encouragement is required
A firm push, when hesitation holds back.
The compass that points away from wrongdoing,
Ideas that guide to accomplishments fulfilling.
Sleepless nights and watchful days,
All needs met, tantrums patiently stayed.
A sounding board for ideas new.
A confidant like whom there are few.

Fierce protector, loyal supporter in trouble
Woe betide all who her feathers ruffle.

Love, fealty, selfless faith in her word and deed,
Only she can encompass all in a beat.
She, masterpiece, a creation like no other,
God's face on earth. Mother.